Rock On! A Look at Geology

Mighty Minerals

Christine Petersen

ABDO Publishing Company

visit us at
www.abdopublishing.com

Published by ABDO Publishing Company, 8000 West 78th Street, Edina, Minnesota 55439.
Copyright © 2010 by Abdo Consulting Group, Inc. International copyrights reserved in all countries.
No part of this book may be reproduced in any form without written permission from the publisher.
The Checkerboard Library™ is a trademark and logo of ABDO Publishing Company.

Printed in the United States of America, North Mankato, Minnesota.
092009
012010

 PRINTED ON RECYCLED PAPER

Cover Photo: Photo Researchers
Interior Photos: Alamy pp. 12, 22, 23; Andrew Silver/U.S. Geological Survey p. 16; AP Images p. 13;
    Getty Images pp. 8, 20, 23, 25, 26–27; iStockphoto pp. 4, 14–15, 17, 18, 19, 23, 27;
    Photo Researchers pp. 1, 19, 21, 24, 28–29; Photolibrary p. 5; U.S. Geological Survey p. 16

Series Coordinator: Megan M. Gunderson
Editors: Heidi M.D. Elston, Megan M. Gunderson
Art Direction & Cover Design: Neil Klinepier

Library of Congress Cataloging-in-Publication Data

Petersen, Christine.
  Mighty minerals / Christine Petersen.
     p. cm. -- (Rock on! A look at geology)
  Includes index.
  ISBN 978-1-60453-744-4
  1. Minerals--Juvenile literature. I. Title.
  QE365.2.P48 2010
  549--dc22
                                    2009027727

Contents

Minerals Are Everywhere!

Anne and her family were enjoying their summer vacation. They took a trip to the beach. There, the sand was warm on Anne's feet. It sparkled as it caught the sunlight. The tiny grains slipped through her fingers as easily as water.

Sand contains minerals.

The next day, Anne's family drove inland. The highway followed a river that flowed past green farm fields. Soon, they were winding up a steep road. The family set up camp in a valley alongside the river. The water flowed around big boulders. Mountain peaks towered high above them.

These places may seem very different. But they have something in common. Much of the beach sand is made up of tiny pieces of minerals. The farm field soil is also full of minerals. Even the huge, towering mountains are made from many minerals packed together.

All minerals have four things in common. Minerals are made in nature, and they are usually **inorganic**. Minerals are also solid substances that each have a specific chemical makeup. Finally, minerals form units called crystals. These features will help you recognize the minerals that surround you!

Earth is covered in rocks made of minerals.

Atoms and Elements

Have you ever played with wooden blocks or construction kits? You can put the pieces together in countless ways. You can make flat surfaces or even **three-dimensional** shapes!

Everything on Earth is made of tiny building blocks called atoms. Bonds are what hold atoms together. In minerals, atoms bond together in a repeating pattern. This forms crystals, which grow larger as more atoms join the pattern.

The pattern of atoms inside every mineral crystal gives it its shape. Crystals of the same mineral have the same shape. Different minerals have different shapes.

Elements are made up of atoms of only one kind. Scientists have discovered more than 100 different elements. Atoms of those elements bond in different patterns and combinations. Together, they produce more than 3,000 known minerals.

Most minerals contain two or more elements. The mineral gypsum is probably in your home in drywall or cement. It contains the elements calcium, sulfur, oxygen, and hydrogen. Tourmaline is a mineral that is often used in jewelry. It can include more than seven different elements.

A few minerals contain only one element. Gold is made of the element gold. Diamond also contains just one element. It is made from carbon.

PERIODIC TABLE OF ELEMENTS

1 H																	2 He
3 Li	4 Be											5 B	6 C	7 N	8 O	9 F	10 Ne
11 Na	12 Mg											13 Al	14 Si	15 P	16 S	17 Cl	18 Ar
19 K	20 Ca	21 Sc	22 Ti	23 V	24 Cr	25 Mn	26 Fe	27 Co	28 Ni	29 Cu	30 Zn	31 Ga	32 Ge	33 As	34 Se	35 Br	36 Kr
37 Rb	38 Sr	39 Y	40 Zr	41 Nb	42 Mo	43 Tc	44 Ru	45 Rh	46 Pd	47 Ag	48 Cd	49 In	50 Sn	51 Sb	52 Te	53 I	54 Xe
55 Cs	56 Ba		72 Hf	73 Ta	74 W	75 Re	76 Os	77 Ir	78 Pt	79 Au	80 Hg	81 Tl	82 Pb	83 Bi	84 Po	85 At	86 Rn
87 Fr	88 Ra		104 Rf	105 Db	106 Sg	107 Bh	108 Hs	109 Mt	110 Ds	111 Rg							

57 La	58 Ce	59 Pr	60 Nd	61 Pm	62 Sm	63 Eu	64 Gd	65 Tb	66 Dy	67 Ho	68 Er	69 Tm	70 Yb	71 Lu
89 Ac	90 Th	91 Pa	92 U	93 Np	94 Pu	95 Am	96 Cm	97 Bk	98 Cf	99 Es	100 Fm	101 Md	102 No	103 Lr

Scientists arrange chemical elements on a chart called the periodic table. Elements are organized into columns, rows, and colors by features they share. Each element has a chemical symbol made up of at least one letter. Some are easy to figure out, while others are not. For example, *O* stands for oxygen. *Pb* stands for lead. The symbol comes from *plumbum*, the Latin word for "lead." When scientists discover new elements, they are added to the table. Each receives a name and a symbol.

Crystal Systems

A mineral crystal's shape is based on how its atoms are arranged. Scientists have fit all these different shapes into six groups called crystal systems. These are isometric, hexagonal, tetragonal, orthorhombic, monoclinic, and triclinic.

The simplest isometric crystals form cubes. The mineral pyrite is isometric. Pyrite is commonly called fool's gold. This is because it can be mistaken for real gold.

Hexagonal crystals may have 6 or 12 sides. They can look like columns or double pyramids. Graphite is a hexagonal mineral. It is used in pencils.

Tetragonal crystals may have four rectangular sides. Squares then form the top and the bottom. Chalcopyrite is a tetragonal mineral. It is a major source of the metal copper.

Fluorite belongs to the isometric crystal system.

Some orthorhombic crystals are made of three pairs of differently shaped rectangles. Others look like two pyramids stuck together. The orthorhombic mineral topaz is a popular gem used in jewelry.

The simplest monoclinic crystals consist of four rectangles and two **rhombuses**. People have long used the monoclinic mineral jadeite for sculptures and jewelry.

Triclinic crystals often look crooked. Their sides have different shapes and do not meet at right angles. Some feldspar minerals are triclinic. Feldspar minerals make up a large part of Earth's crust.

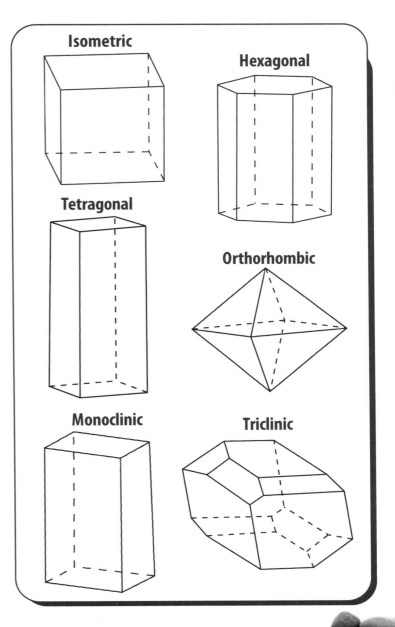

Isometric

Hexagonal

Tetragonal

Orthorhombic

Monoclinic

Triclinic

Make Rock Candy!

What You'll Need

- cotton string • pencil
- paper clip • glass jar
- medium saucepan
- 3 1/2 cups granulated sugar
- 1 cup water • food coloring

What You'll Do

1. Ask an adult to help you!

2. Measure a piece of cotton string about the height of the jar. Tie one end to the middle of the pencil. Tie the other end to the paper clip.

3. Lay the pencil across the top of the jar. The string should hang about two-thirds of the way down inside the jar.

4. Bring the water to a boil in the saucepan. Add sugar slowly, stirring until it dissolves. This will form a syrup.

5. Add 3 drops of food coloring.

6. Turn off the stove. Let the mixture sit for 30 minutes.

7. Pour the syrup into the jar.

8. Set the jar in a safe place. Crystals will form over the next few days.

9. Once they've grown, pull out the crystal-covered string and take a close look. Sugar may not be a mineral, but its crystals do fit into a specific system. The answer is upside down on the next page!

What crystal system do sugar crystals belong to?

They belong to the monoclinic crystal system.

Mineral Formation

Many minerals grow from liquids, including **magma**. Magma bubbles up from deep below Earth's surface. It may stop before reaching the surface or erupt from volcanoes as lava. As the magma cools and hardens, mineral crystals grow. These crystals harden into igneous rock.

Minerals also form as wind, rain, and ice wear down this rock. Little bits of rock break off, wash away, and gather in a new place. These sediments are made of various minerals. As they pile up, pressure increases and sedimentary rock forms. Some minerals survive this process, while others newly form there.

Granite forms as magma cools slowly underground. It contains large, colorful crystals of the minerals quartz and feldspar.

Halite, or rock salt, is mined from within the earth.

When rocks are under great heat and pressure, new minerals form. Deep underground, those forces turn the rock's old minerals into new ones. These changes also create metamorphic rock.

Minerals also grow when water freezes or dries up. That means ice is a mineral. Its crystals grow when water freezes. Halite crystals form when oceans or salty lakes dry up. Halite is the mineral name for salt. Ancient oceans left behind large amounts of halite around the world. Today, people mine it from underground. Halite is used to melt ice on winter roads and even to make homemade ice cream!

The Rock Cycle

Igneous rock forms as magma cools above or below Earth's surface.

magma

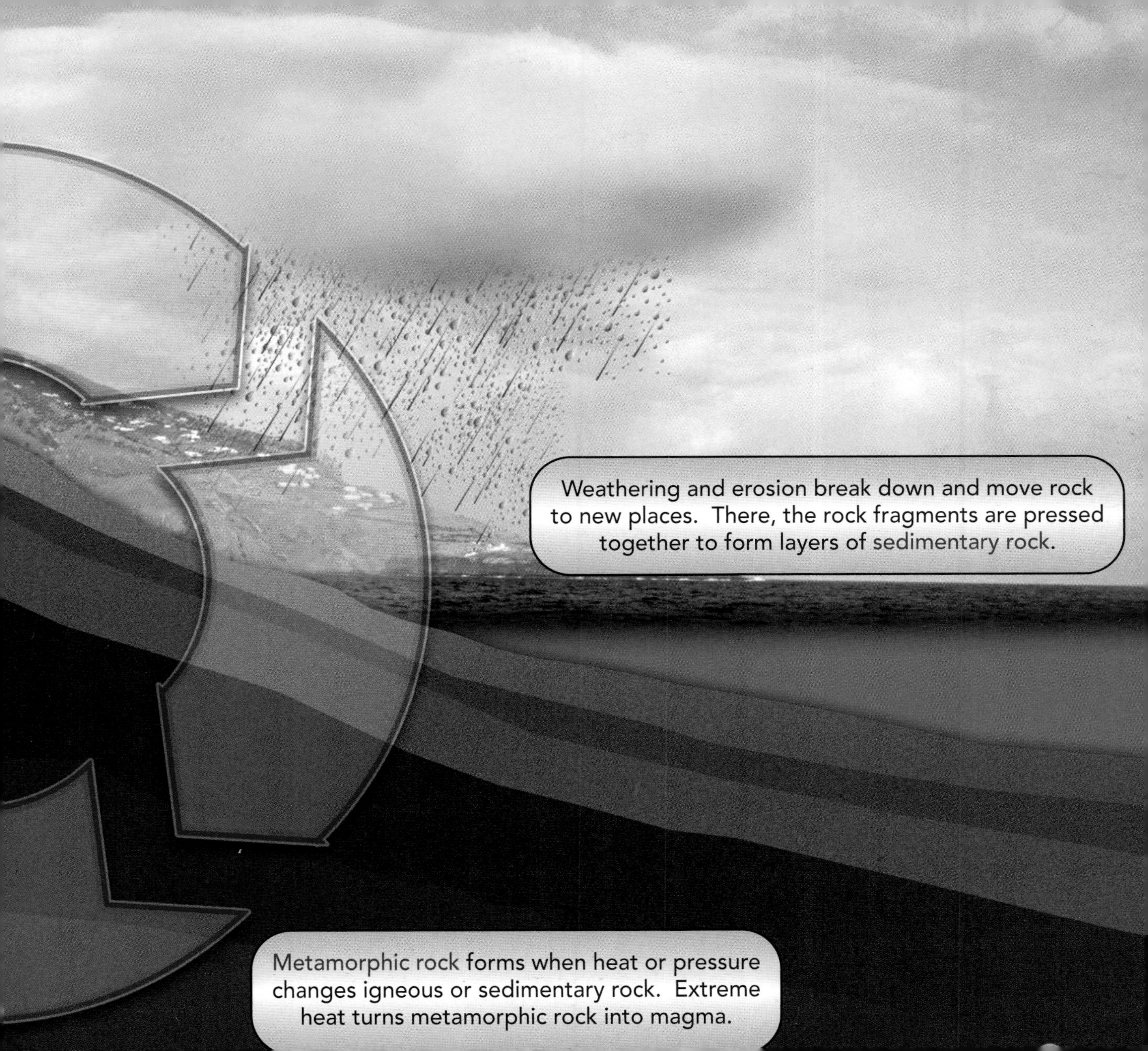

Weathering and erosion break down and move rock to new places. There, the rock fragments are pressed together to form layers of sedimentary rock.

Metamorphic rock forms when heat or pressure changes igneous or sedimentary rock. Extreme heat turns metamorphic rock into magma.

Identifying by Color

It can be hard to identify minerals just by looking at them. So, scientists rely on different physical properties and tests to tell one mineral from another.

Color is one of the most obvious properties of an object. Some minerals occur in only one color. Sulfur is always yellow, and malachite can only be green. So, color helps identify them.

However, many minerals are found in a variety of colors. The

Sulfur

Malachite

mineral corundum is a good example. Pure corundum crystals are colorless. Rare crystals of corundum may be bright blue or red. These are the gemstones known as sapphires and rubies.

The mineral azurite is always blue.

Luster and Streak

Another visual way to identify minerals is luster. Luster describes the way minerals reflect light. Minerals such as pyrite shine like metal. Others are described as glassy, oily, pearly, or dull.

A streak color test is another way to tell minerals apart. Take a slightly rough white **porcelain** tile and scratch the mineral along it. The rubbing leaves behind a powder line of color.

No matter their color, samples of the same mineral have the same streak color. For example, corundum has a white streak no matter what color its crystals are.

Turquoise has a waxy luster.

The mineral galena has a metallic luster.

Hematite (left) varies from red to black. But, its streak is always red. Malachite's streak (right) is always green.

Breaking Minerals

Scientists also study how a mineral breaks to help identify it. Some minerals are softer than others. Diamond is the hardest natural substance on Earth. It forms deep beneath the crust. There, heat and pressure push its atoms close together. They bond strongly to neighbors all around. Yet even the hardest minerals can break.

A smooth break is called cleavage. Minerals that cleave break into pieces with flat surfaces. They also break in certain directions. Diamond breaks in four directions to make pyramid shapes. Halite breaks into cubes. Mica has perfect cleavage. It breaks into thin layers like sheets of paper.

Some crystals do not break into pieces with flat, even surfaces. Instead, they fracture. Quartz is a mineral that does this. It is a very hard mineral that is common in Earth's crust. When

Mica

quartz breaks, it has smooth, curved surfaces like a shell. Other minerals fracture in different ways. They may break into splintery fragments or become hackly, or jagged.

Citrine is a form of quartz. So when it breaks, its surfaces are not flat.

Hardness and Density

Hardness is yet another way to identify a mineral. In the early 1800s, German scientist Friedrich Mohs created a scale of mineral hardness. The scale has values from one to ten. One is the softest, and ten is the hardest.

Mohs chose one mineral to represent each value on the scale. Hardness is determined by whether or not a mineral can scratch one of these ten minerals. A harder mineral can scratch a softer mineral.

A few everyday objects are also used on the scale. Some minerals are soft enough to be scratched by a

By scratching one mineral against another, scientists can tell which one is harder.

1 **2** **3** **4** **5**

copper penny. Their hardness is three or lower. Other minerals are too hard to be scratched by a pocketknife. Their hardness is six or higher.

Scientists also use specific gravity to identify minerals. Specific gravity compares a mineral's weight against the weight of the same volume of water. For example, graphite has a specific gravity of 2.23. It is more than twice as heavy as water. Diamond has a specific gravity of 3.51. Gold and platinum are very heavy. They can have a specific gravity higher than 19!

MOHS HARDNESS SCALE

	Mohs Hardness	Mineral	Hardness of Other Materials
SOFTEST	1	talc	
	2	gypsum	2.2 fingernail
	3	calcite	3.2 copper penny
	4	fluorite	
↓	5	apatite	5.1 pocketknife
	6	orthoclase	5.5 glass plate
HARDEST	7	quartz	6.5 steel needle
	8	topaz	7.0 streak plate
	9	corundum	
	10	diamond	

6 **7** **8** **9** **10**

Magical Minerals?

A few minerals are easy to identify because they have very special features. Some minerals that contain iron have magnetic properties. Magnetite and pyrrhotite share this feature. They are both attracted to magnets. Magnets attract iron, nickel, steel, and other objects. Magnetite can also act as a magnet.

Magnetite will attract objects such as paper clips.

Another special feature some minerals have is fluorescence. Fluorite crystals are a good example of this. In normal white light, they can appear yellow, orange, black, pink, brown, green, or purple. Yet under special **ultraviolet** light, fluorite crystals usually glow blue or green!

Calcite minerals have red fluorescence. The mineral zircon can contain traces of the element manganese. When it does, it fluoresces yellow under ultraviolet light.

The minerals calcite (red) *and willemite* (green) *show fluorescence.*

Putting Minerals to Work

People have used minerals for thousands of years. Today, we can't live without them. Take a quick look around your house. You might be surprised by how many objects contain minerals.

The coins in your piggy bank are made from minerals such as copper. Some toothpastes and drinking water contain fluoride, which helps reduce tooth decay. Fluoride contains a substance that comes from the mineral fluorite.

People have been using the mineral graphite in pencils for hundreds of years.

Quartz can be melted down to make window glass. Lenses for telescopes and microscopes are also made from quartz crystals. And, quartz crystals are used in watches. The crystals vibrate a certain number of times per second. The watch uses this to help measure time.

Metals can also be minerals. Iron is a strong metal. It can be made into steel

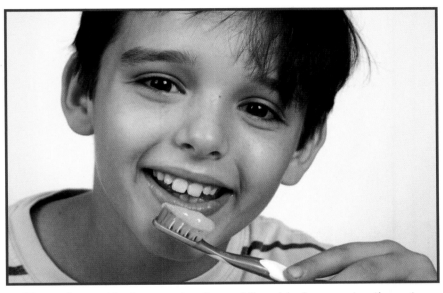

There is apatite in your teeth and fluoride in your toothpaste. They help keep your teeth strong and healthy.

and used to make buildings and bridges. Water pipes are often made from copper, which does not rust.

There are even minerals inside living things. Apatite is a mineral found in your body. It forms part of your teeth and bones. Apatite represents a five on the Mohs hardness scale.

Change Happens

Earth is a place where things are always changing. Minerals are forming and breaking down all around us. They are even growing deep underground in caves.

For thousands of years, crystals grew in Mexico's Cave of Crystals. A mineral from water in the cave **dissolved** to form gypsum. Over time, this formed gigantic gypsum crystals up to 36 feet (11 m) long! Today, they are some of the largest natural crystals ever found.

Minerals are found everywhere. Yet many are found only in small amounts. Mining them from the ground can be damaging to the planet. So, we must use minerals wisely. That way, they will continue to improve our lives long into the future. The next time you visit the beach or the mountains, remember all the minerals that surround you!

Cave of Crystals

Glossary

dissolve - to pass into solution or become liquid.

inorganic - being or made of matter other than plant or animal.

magma - melted rock beneath Earth's surface.

porcelain - a hard, fine-grained, transparent and white material.

rhombus - a shape with four equal sides and sometimes no right angles.

three-dimensional - having three dimensions, such as length, width, and height.

ultraviolet - a type of light that cannot be seen with the human eye.

Saying It

chalcopyrite - kal-kuh-PEYE-rite
fluorescence - flu-REH-suhns
Friedrich Mohs - FREE-drihk MOHS
igneous - IHG-nee-uhs
malachite - MA-luh-kite
manganese - MANG-guh-neez
metamorphic - meh-tuh-MAWR-fihk
orthorhombic - awr-thuh-RAHM-bihk
porcelain - PAWR-suh-luhn
pyrrhotite - PIHR-uh-tite
rhombus - RAHM-buhs
sapphire - SA-fire
turquoise - TUHR-koyz

Web Sites

To learn more about minerals, visit ABDO Publishing Company on the World Wide Web at **www.abdopublishing.com**. Web sites about minerals are featured on our Book Links page. These links are routinely monitored and updated to provide the most current information available.

Index